A Harmonious Path for Buddhist Communities

A Harmonious Path for Buddhist Communities

Advice on Keeping Amiable Relations Within a Dharma Center

by Khenpo Sherap Phuntsok

translated by Michele Martin

KTD Publications
Woodstock New York USA

KTD Publications
335 Meads Mountain Road
Woodstock, New York

ISBN: 978-1-934608-34-0

Printed in the United States on 100% PCR,
acid-free paper

Contents

We must examine again and again
The state of our mind and body.
This in itself is a brief definition
Of remaining mindful and alert.

Shantideva, *The Way of a Bodhisattva*,
Chapter Five, verse 108

Advice on Keeping Amiable Relations Within a Dharma Center

I pay homage to the lama and to the mind of awakening. As they spread from India to Tibet, the Buddha's teachings preserved their blessings, which have continued down to this very day as the Dharma is branching out to the East and West. This expansion is due to the Buddha's bodhicitta and the kindness of great lamas who have come to benefit others and the teachings. Also, at the root of this development are the lamas and disciples, whose kindness, aspirations, and activities have created Dharma centers in so many countries. At these homes for the Dharma, it is extremely important that relationships be harmonious and Vajrayana commitments be kept. And so, as if giving advice to friends, with the best of intentions, I have put down some thoughts about how those involved with Dharma centers can work well together.

Note: In the following pages, the word *lama* appears in referring to a teacher. Though the word is from the Tibetan, the advice is meant to apply to the wide variety of Buddhist centers found throughout the world.

The Foundation of an Excellent Motivation

A good motivation must be present from the beginning. It is at the very foundation of the relationships between a Dharma center's lama and students. This good intention must also underlie the thought of starting a Dharma center. What is the real purpose of creating one? We and all others wish for happiness but may not know that practicing Dharma is the virtuous activity that brings it about. Although we do not wish for suffering, in the natural course of things, we engage in unvirtuous and negative activity that causes suffering. So what we wish for and what we actually do run counter to each other. Dharma centers are started so that we can enter the gate of the Buddha's precious teachings and then blend the Dharma into our own experience. In particular, we can do the practice of a deity with whom we have a special karmic connection. On the basis of practicing true Dharma, we can attain authentic results on a relative and ultimate level. This is why we start a Dharma center.

With this kind of motivation, creating, maintaining, and developing a Dharma center needs the best of preparations. To give an example, for a fine tree to grow, we first need a seed that is not rotten or defective. Once the seed is planted, conditions that foster growth, such as water, fertilizer, and sunlight, must all be present. Finally, if a fruit does not ripen, then having planted the seed would be useless; it's crucial to have a result from all our labors.

If good results are not forthcoming, disciples might think that the Dharma center exists for the lama's sake or merely for making connections and getting to know one another in passing. The lamas should be thinking about benefitting others through the genuine Dharma and helping them in other ways as well. Otherwise, the lamas might think that the center is just providing them with a good living situation or a way to make a name for themselves. They might even think that it doesn't matter whether the students are helped by the Dharma or not. If we hold such impure motivations, it is really difficult for us to find a true purpose in starting a Dharma center and for it to develop fully. Thus, for many reasons, these kinds of negative motivations should be dropped, and both the lama and the disciples must definitely have the good intention that is at the heart of relationships.

What then is the result of a good motivation? If we can create a well-organized and developed center, then those who wish to practice can open their eyes to see what they should and should not do. They will know that practicing Dharma is the cause of happiness and also that they should abandon negative and unvirtuous activity, the very cause of suffering. Once the afflictions within their mindstream have been tamed, the sun of well-being and happiness will shine forth because they have found this excellent opportunity to practice Dharma.

Furthermore, they can also help other members of the sangha, who are the very foundation of the teachings and who engage in vast and excellent activities. When the sangha prospers, there are many positive results. In terms of the scriptures, what flourishes are explanations of the teachings, debate about them, and composition as well as study, contemplation, and meditation. In terms of realization, the practice of the three trainings—discipline, wisdom, and samadhi—will unfold. Through all of this, many living beings will experience increased well-being and happiness.

For these numerous reasons, it is crucial that in the beginning, middle, and end both the lama and the disciples rely on an excellent motivation, the basis for everything positive.

The Importance of Trust

For a good relationship to develop between lamas and disciples, the disciples must first examine carefully and think clearly about their relationship with the lama because it is crucial.

Once we have taken a particular lama as our teacher, the lama and student must trust each other. Without trust, no genuine Dharma or useful activities can be accomplished. For example, when lamas are teaching Dharma and giving advice, if the students do not trust them, they will also not trust the path of Dharma being taught and consequently, will not enter it. If this happens, their relationship will become remote and Dharma activities will not unfold. This is looking at the situation from the student's perspective.

From the lama's perspective, if he or she does not trust the disciples who are participating in Dharma activities and sincerely supporting the Dharma center, the lama will not give them recognition or positive support and the students will lose heart. In this way, too, the relationship of lama and disciple grows distant and the Dharma center cannot progress.

When the Buddha was teaching the genuine Dharma, his followers entered the path knowing well the reasons for doing so. Through trusting the path and engaging in practice, they attained a positive result. Those who had doubts about the Buddha's Dharma did not enter the path and, of course, did not find an authentic result.

The Importance of Being Kind and Loving to Each Other

The lamas in Dharma centers should be kind and loving to their students, thinking, "I will benefit them in this life and lives to come." With compassion they should think, "Some disciples are experiencing suffering—a temporary illness, mental discomfort, or profound misery. Through the Dharma, I will find a way to free them from their sickness and suffering." Practicing compassion like this, the lamas should be kind and loving to their students. The students should also be kind and loving to their lamas. When the lamas are putting their hearts into benefitting the teachings and living beings, the students should think, "To fulfill their wishes, I will help my spiritual friend. With love and kindness, I will support and contribute to this work in whatever way I can." When the lama is ill or dealing with a difficult situation, the disciples should think with compassion, "Using all possible means, I will help as best I can to overcome these difficulties." It is crucial that lamas and students are kind and loving to one another.

What is the result of being kind and loving?

If the relationship between lama and disciple is free of resentment, aversion, and other negative emotions, they will be able to engage in Dharma work with joy and delight, like a swan gliding into a lake of lotus flowers. Also, the lama's purpose in coming to stay at the center will be fulfilled. It is just like a household. If the family members relate to each other with a mind filled with love and kindness, they all will be happy and thriving.

THE NEED FOR GOOD RELATIONSHIPS

A lama is someone who thinks from the perspective of the student. Such a spiritual friend can show us the path and answer our questions as we move toward full awakening. It is very important, therefore, to honor and respect the lama. In relying on a spiritual friend, we are able to ask questions about what we don't know or have doubts about. Then when we practice Dharma with our doubts resolved, we can be at ease and free of worry. If we do not depend on a spiritual friend, when we start practice, we will not have true confidence nor the courage that comes from being totally assured. Our doubts and misconceptions will gradually multiply, and there's a danger that our practice will not progress along the path.

For example, if the keeper of a garden, filled with fruits and flowers, looks after it well, abundant flowers will blossom and the fruits will ripen fully. If there is no one to care for the garden, to give it water and fertilizer, it will go to seed and disappear. In this example, the lama is the gardener and the disciples are the trees and flowers. Similarly, when traveling a long distance, if we have a guide and a courageous escort to protect us, we can journey with an easy mind, free of fear and doubts about the way. A true spiritual friend is a guide like this, who helps our Dharma practice progress along the path. It's crucial, therefore, to foster this relationship in harmony with the Dharma and rely on the lama with genuine respect.

The purpose of the Buddha's teaching is to bring well-being and happiness to others. When the lama is creating a connection with disciples, it is the lama's responsibility to care for them with kindness and love. At that time, in the eyes of the disciples, the lama's demeanor should be pleasant and evoke a joyful feeling, free of anything discordant or troubling. The lama's speech should be pleasant to hear. The Buddha taught four ways for teachers to gather disciples: being generous, speaking pleasantly, encouraging meaningful behavior, and consistency between words and deeds. Through training in these four, lamas can benefit others.

When lamas and disciples have a good relationship, streams of people will enter the gate of Dharma and discover the numerous qualities of this path leading to liberation and omniscience. This is how the Buddha's teachings can flourish. And having begun to practice Dharma, these disciples will also experience Dharma moving along the path without adversity or obstacles. Rather than wasting their lives in meaningless activity, which they will later regret, they will be confident that they have given meaning to the leisures and resources of this life and lives to come.

THE WHEEL OF ACTIVITY

When we are serving the Buddha's teachings, there are three main activities we can do: understand the teachings, maintain them, and spread them. To understand the teachings means to study and contemplate the three sections, or pitaka, of the scriptures (the vinaya, sutra, and abhidharma) and to practice the path of the three trainings (discipline, wisdom, and samadhi). Maintaining the teachings relates to the path of skillful means that allows us to remain continuously in the study, contemplation, and practice just described. Spreading the teachings is the activity of greatly increasing the first two activities, so that the teachings spread out in all directions and become widely available. Of these three, the activity of spreading the teachings is the most important as it includes everything.

There are three successive wheels, or spheres, related to the ways of understanding, maintaining, and spreading the teachings. Reading belongs to the wheel of study and contemplation; discarding what is negative, to the wheel of stable meditation; and activity, to the wheel of work. When we are seeking to understand and maintain the teachings, the first and second wheels are the most important. When we are spreading the teachings of the Buddha, the third wheel of work is the most important. If we just hang back and do not get involved, we cannot expect that the Buddha's teachings will spread by themselves. We need to take part on many levels. When the Dharma finds a home in numerous countries, this is a definite cause for the development of perfect well-being and happiness in this world of ours.

How do we turn this third wheel so that the

Buddha's teachings flourish? In places where the Buddha's teachings are unavailable or in decline, we can build stupas, construct temples, establish Dharma centers, and create places for the sangha. Having studied the teachings, we can introduce others to the Dharma and learn languages to do translation work. In all these ways, we can open the door to the Dharma for many disciples. We can take responsibility for such activities and actually do them. Or, when others are engaged in them, we can help by creating favorable conditions and endeavoring to assist them in any way we can with our body, speech, and mind.

The Need to Be Direct and Truthful

When we are working in Dharma centers or engaged in any activity related to Dharma, it is extremely important to be direct and truthful, free of duplicity and deceit. If we are not straightforward and honest about small things, other people might not sense it right away, but one day they will see what we have kept hidden. Then later, when we want to accomplish a large undertaking and actually do speak directly, it could happen that others cannot trust or depend on us. If others have no confidence in our project, we cannot succeed. Further, if we are not direct and truthful, our lama, fellow practitioners, and others will dislike us. If we don't know how to be in harmony with others, then even when we sincerely come up with a good idea, not only will we not be able to help the Dharma center in any significant way, we won't even be able to help ourselves or others in general.

Turning this around, if we are forthright

and open in matters both small and great , our lama and all our Dharma friends will trust us. With this trust, we will be able to serve the Dharma center in many ways, and through the Dharma, bring great benefit to people in general as well as our own Dharma friends. On a personal level, we can learn and profit a great deal through our experience: for example, we will know how to practice genuine Dharma; we will be a person others can trust; our words will be valuable; and we will know how to serve the Dharma and other living beings.

The Importance of a Good Motivation Before Any Activity

Whatever we are doing, whether we are engaging in Dharma activity or personal projects, it is essential to be imbued with a positive motivation. When we begin any activity that involves our body or speech, if our motivation is based on the afflictions—excessive desire, aversion, dullness, pride, jealousy, and so on—what we are doing mutates into a negative and unvirtuous action. On the other hand, if we begin with a positive intention, filled with love and compassion and the wish to help others, then what we're doing becomes virtuous. Not coming under the power of the afflictions and not falling prey to a mistaken motivation, we can cultivate a good one by thinking that our activity helps to spread the Buddha's teachings and that through our work, the great good of genuine Dharma comes to many. We can develop a mind that yearns to benefit others to the best of our ability. If others are not happy mentally, if they are miserable, hard-pressed, or filled with worry, we can seek to help them through actually doing something ourselves, or we can show them the skillful means of relying on a good lama. We need to train in cultivating these excellent intentions, bringing them to mind often throughout the hours of the day.

In the beginning, it is difficult to give rise to even a small positive intention. However, if over a few years, we can make an intensive effort to remain mindful, alert, and conscious, then gradually, we will naturally and easily be able to generate an excellent motivation, which will also appear more frequently. And the benefits do not stop here. In this life, if we can train to have a good attitude, then having placed this imprint in our mind, in future lives we can take a special rebirth in the form of a kindhearted person. This happens because karma, the linking of cause and effect, is certain.

Developing Our Motivation to Engage in the Dharma

The main objective in creating a center is to spread the Dharma so that many people and other beings may be benefitted. And it goes without saying that those who come to the center do so for the sake of the genuine Dharma and, therefore, their motivation is also turned toward the Dharma. Nonetheless, due to the presence of powerful habits ingrained from beginningless time, our motivation is mixed with a steady focus on ourselves. Pride, jealousy, and other afflictions are also mixed in, so our activity becomes worldly. We can know this from our own experience. When our motivation deviates like this, if we just leave it as it is and do not set it right, the power of our tainted intentions will increase.

So we may be saying, "This is Dharma activity," but these are mere words; in fact, our activity has turned into a worldly one.

For all these reasons, when we are starting out on a Dharma project, if we are mindful and alert, and at the same time our mind is imbued with the correct motivation, then our activity will truly harmonize with the Dharma and bring benefit to many others. A positive motivation is also valuable in other ways: whatever we undertake will be successful and the result will find its fruition without big obstacles or difficulties.

There is a story from the time of the Buddha. Along with the sangha of fully ordained monks, he was once invited for a meal at the home of a sponsor. Two others seeking alms also appeared—a young man belonging to the royal caste and another to the brahmin caste.

The Brahmin youth went in to beg before food was offered to the Buddha and his retinue, so he received nothing. The royal youth waited until everyone had been served, then received food, enjoyed it, and left having experienced many delicious things. As the two were later walking along the road and conversing, the royal youth said, "If I had wealth and resources, throughout my life, I would serve and honor the Buddha and his followers by offering food and alms." The Brahmin youth said, "If I had power as the king of a country, I would behead all those ordained monks along with their followers."

The royal youth then traveled to another country and sat in the shade of a large tree. The shadows cast by other trees passed away, but the shadow where the royal youth was sitting did not move. At this time, the king of the country died without an heir, and the people decided to appoint as their king someone who had great merit and who could exert a powerful influence. The people looked everywhere and finally came upon the royal youth asleep under the tree that had kept its shadow unchanged from morning to afternoon. When he awoke, the people asked him to be their king. Later, according to his previous wishes, he made offerings to the Buddha and his retinue. The Brahmin youth, however, was sleeping one day at the side of a road when a carriage swerved from its path, rolled over his neck, and beheaded him. This traditional story is used to illustrate the importance of having a good motivation, free of error and turned toward the Dharma.

How do we increase our positive motivation? We should think in terms of the many lives to come rather than focusing on this life alone. Why? In practicing the Dharma, it is possible to find well-being, happiness, and freedom from worry. But Dharma practice is not just for this life; it is really for all our lives to come, so that we can find the joy of higher rebirths as gods and humans and, ultimately, liberation and omniscience. We could use Dharma to seek comfort and happiness in this life, to wile away our time in pleasant talk, to seek fame, and so forth, but this is not the Dharma that will bring us along the path. From the outside we may appear to be a Dharma practitioner, but actually there's a great danger that what we're doing is not much different from worldly activity.

If we look inside and really think about it, we can see that this life is just one life and that future lives will not be just one or two but continue for a very long time. It is easy to see that what happens for a considerable number of lives is more important than what happens in just one. Therefore, whenever we use our body, speech, and mind, we should rely on being mindful, alert, and careful so that we don't fall prey to our afflictions or carelessness. Through skillfully monitoring the behavior of our body, speech, and mind, if we can alter our life so that we spend 80 percent of our time for the sake of future lives, our Dharma practice will go well.

How to Speak with Others

Once we've joined a Dharma center and are engaged in its work, the way we speak determines whether the connections we make in communicating with others will go well or not. Therefore, it is important to know how to speak well. The protector Nagarjuna said that there are various ways of speaking—honey-like words, flower-like words, and offensive words.

What is meant by "honey-like words"? Though words do not have the sharp and jagged edge of a knife, if we do not know how to express ourselves, we can cut a person's mind to pieces. Avoiding very rough words that bring misery and distress to others, those skilled in speaking use pleasant-sounding words; rather than pointless gossip, they talk about what is meaningful; and they choose words that create delight, happiness, and joy. Just like honey, the taste of such words is delicious and pleasing to everyone.

The second type of words are like flowers. What we say is not tainted by lies but simply remains direct and open. In this way, what is said is beautiful; whoever hears it finds nothing untoward, so the words slip into their minds. Usually, if we speak only the truth whenever we talk, all of our words, however many there may be, are experienced as beautiful and full of meaning, so others consider them interesting and valuable. For example, the shape and color of a flower are beautiful and appeal to everyone.

The third type of works are offensive words—harsh words that provoke anger when heard, or words that are not straightforward and truthful. Offensive words also refer to talk that is mixed with praising ourselves and putting down others, or talk that is mingled with deception and hypocrisy. Just as a foul smell is repulsive to everyone—rich or poor, high or low—if we speak in harsh and offensive ways that disturb another's mind, everyone will find it unpleasant. There's also the danger that others will dislike us and turn against us.

As the bodhisattva Shantideva wrote in *Entering the Way of a Bodhisattva:*

> When speaking, use words relevant
> and agreeable,
> Pleasant to hear and with their meaning
> clear,
> Free of attachment and free of hate,
> Speak with gentleness and
> moderation.

Therefore, among the three ways to speak, we should use the first two, the honey-like and flower-like words, while also staying mindful, alert, and conscious.

THE IMPORTANCE OF PRACTICING PATIENCE

Whether we're doing Dharma or worldly work, it can never be completely free of faults. So when things so wrong and become unpleasant or don't go our way, it is of great benefit to practice a patience grounded in being mindful and alert. When we can't find our patience in the midst of difficulty, we could, for example, allow anger to arise. Anger creates distress, causes fighting, and can even disturb our sleep. So we should use all the skillful means we know and do everything in our power to keep anger from rearing its head. It is said that having fine-tuned our awareness, we should seize the weapon of being mindful and alert to quash anger as soon as it arises. Protecting ourselves this way is crucial.

Actually, if we really examine a situation, we can see that there is no good reason to be angry. Again from *Entering the Way of a Bodhisattva:*

> If it can be fixed,
> Why dislike it?
> If it can't be fixed,
> What's the use of dislike?

If something goes wrong in our work and it can be fixed, then feeling dislike or getting angry about it will not get the job done. If we look for a method to correct the mistake, we can finish our project successfully and accomplish something very useful. On the other hand, if it cannot be fixed, how could dislike or anger help? They're of no use at all. Instead, if we can practice a little patience, we will gather powerful merit. Therefore, we should earnestly apply ourselves to dealing with our afflictions.

Especially when we are working in a Dharma center, we must pay careful attention to the methods that prevent anger from arising. Why? Almost all of us who are active in Dharma centers have the same spiritual friend as a teacher; we practice Dharma together; and we hold commitments as brothers and sisters in the Vajrayana. So if we get angry and attack each other, there is a great danger of impairing our vows and commitments. This fault is different from others and more serious.

Since Dharma-center work is for the sake of the Buddha's teachings, for the monasteries, and for the well-being and happiness of others, if we get furious and fight, we are creating huge obstacles to the work. This runs counter to the advice we received on taking refuge vows. We are also discarding the Dharma and turning away from helping others. These are serious mistakes, so it is critical that within a state that is mindful and alert, we use vigorous means to prevent anger from arising. In addition to all these negative consequences, once anger has arisen, our minds are disturbed and we cannot accomplish anything, large or small.

The bodhisattva Shantideva writes:

> Practiced for thousands of aeons, our
> generosity
> In offering to the Sugatas and others,
> All the fine things we have done,
> Are effaced in an instant of anger.

All the accumulations of virtue and merit we have gathered for hundreds of thousands of aeons are obliterated by a moment's anger. For this reason, we must be extremely careful that it does not arise.

An antidote for anger is practicing patience. Bringing to mind the benefits of patience increases our eagerness to meditate on it and our ability to do so. What are the benefits of patience? When we are practicing patience, negative emotions, such as hatred and dislike, do not have a chance to appear so we can remain peaceful and relaxed. In this state of mind, we can get things done without obstacles. Others who look at us with negative intentions—seeking to harm us, wishing us ill, or just disliking us—will drop them. Gradually mutual affection and kindness will develop, and due to this, authentic Dharma practice will arise in both of us. If we can meditate well on patience, we'll have the reputation of a good and agreeable person. These are a few of the numerous benefits that the practice of patience brings.

Traditionally, it is said that being generous and maintaining discipline (the first two of the six perfections) bring vast merit, but even more excellent is practicing patience (the third perfection). According to the Buddha, the virtue and its causes that come from practicing the six perfections increase in excellence as we progress from the first to the sixth one.

The Obstacle of Self-Centeredness

Self-centeredness, pride, jealousy, and competitiveness are the main culprits that make obstacles for whatever work we may do. We need great vigilance in dealing with all of them. First of all, we need to pay careful attention to our self-centered mind. When we are engaged in beneficial activity—spreading the teachings of the Buddha, serving the sangha, looking after the poor, or listening, reflecting, and meditating on the Dharma—we should cast aside the frame of mind that is set on making things go well for ourselves and instead place others front and center. If we can keep this in mind, then our work becomes truly beneficial to the teachings and to all forms of life.

By contrast, placing ourselves at stage center runs contrary to the bodhisattva's way. Work done with such an attitude is merely self-serving and cannot bring a significant benefit to a lot of people. If our efforts are to turn out well, we must cut off thinking so much about ourselves and shine the spotlight on others. From *Entering the Way of a Bodhisattva:*

"If I give this away, what will I use?"
Thinking of me, the mean-spirited way.
"If I use it, what will I have to give?"
Thinking of others, the Dharma divine.

How to understand this? If we have something very nice and give it away with the thought, "What will I use now?" that is thinking mainly of our own benefit. Shantideva calls this "the mean-spirited way." But thinking, "If I myself use this wonderful thing, what will I have to give others?" he calls the divine motivation, which is focused on benefitting others. If we have not yet developed this, we can practice a kind of alchemy. The mind fixated on ourselves is like iron; if we add the mercury of Shantideva's advice, it will transform this mind into the gold of bodhicitta, the best motivation.

THE OBSTACLE OF PRIDE

When we are doing good works, we should be on the lookout for pride. If Dharma practitioners really think about it, they will see that there's a need to closely monitor pride. It is said that the water of good qualities does not adhere to a mass of pride. When someone's mind is all puffed up with arrogance, it resembles a large lump, and good qualities cannot enter the mindstream of such a person. When we are receiving teachings or an initiation from a lama, we first make three prostrations to expel pride from our mind. If we're overproud, then even when we're doing some minor job, we wind up bragging and showing off to others. Since this makes them dislike us, we cannot carry out our worthwhile projects.

Also when we're studying hard, if we develop a lot of pride, we will not find a good teacher to explain the texts. Or if we do find one, since we are overconfident and don't study much, pride will prevent our studies from progressing. Likewise, when we are practicing genuine Dharma and find the small tip of a good quality, such as the appearance of signs or marks, we cannot keep our mind placed on what we're experiencing, because our experience is swamped by a wave of pride. When this happens, it shows that obstacles, or maras (negative spirits), have found their perch. They will definitely prevent the qualities of meditative experience and realization from arising. Discussions about how this can happen are found in many texts: in the life stories of past lamas, commentaries, and key instructions for practice. In a sum, no matter what kind of Dharma we are practicing to benefit ourselves and others, it's essential to be free of pride.

The Obstacle of Jealousy

When we are involved in good projects, it's important that we also be free of jealousy. With Dharma activity we benefit others and refrain from harming them. But when jealousy raises its head, it disturbs and upsets people. In this way, we create barriers and obstacles for each other and end up benefitting neither ourselves nor others. On top of this, if fighting breaks out, there's the danger of becoming enemies.

In particular, when we are engaged in Dharma-center activity, if we dislike or are jealous of each other and show it through our demeanor, then our Dharma center's work will unravel; the students will not be able to keep their Vajrayana commitments (samayas), and their relationship with the lama will be disturbed. Due to all of this, the lama will face great difficulties. So jealousy brings tremendous harm to the teachings and to living beings.

In stark contrast to this, when free of jealousy, we can meditate on rejoicing in others' activity whatever it may be, and help them as much as we can. When this is possible, our projects and others' will be effortlessly accomplished and we will really be able to help. For example, it is said that unable to stand the abundant prosperity of the gods, the demigods become jealous and have to undergo the suffering of continual fighting. On the other hand, the gods are not jealous of each other's fortune, so they always enjoy well-being and happiness.

The Obstacle of Competitiveness

In general, a certain amount of healthy competition can improve what we're doing. For example, when two countries compete in sports, their game can improve. However, when our efforts are for the Dharma, this type of motivation is quite mistaken: it is not in harmony with the Dharma and runs counter to a bodhisattva's way. Not only that, if we are competitive, we will not feel joy or delight in our work, but go around with our minds upset. Our energy and strength will not be up to the task, and our inability to complete successfully what we have started will cause us embarrassment and useless worry.

Even though we can tap into a tremendous energy for a project, if it turns into a cause for pride and showing off, the work will bring more harm than help. We should uproot such negative motivations and engage in tasks, large or small, that benefit the teachings and all forms of life. In the best case, we are motivated by bodhicitta. If not, then it is essential that we have the good intention of a pure sincerity that does not go against the genuine Dharma.

The Need to Be Conscious of Our Body and Speech

Within organizations like a Dharma center in which many people participate, it is very important to be mindful, alert, and conscious of how we conduct ourselves physically and verbally. Why is this so? Since our body and speech follow after our mind, most people infer how another's mind is from the person's physical and verbal expressions. Even if we have good intentions, if we do not know how to express them through our body and speech, we will not be considered a good person.

The bodhisattva Shantideva writes:

> All that causes others to lose faith
> We abandon by seeing it ourselves or
> asking others.

We should examine to see if what we do physically or verbally might cause others to lose faith, dislike us, or give rise to afflictions and unvirtuous thoughts. We can honestly ask others for feedback and also, using our knowledge of the view, analyze well. In these ways we can see if we have become careless and then, being mindful and alert, set our behavior on the right path again.

When we are with others, if we know how

to move in ways that are acceptable and admirable, we will make a positive impression and become an inspiration for others. In terms of speech, if we are articulate, we can turn people toward the Dharma. Previously, among the five excellent ones (the first disciples of the Buddha), Asvajit carried his body in such a peaceful, disciplined, and conscious way that faith naturally arose in Shariputra and he entered the gate of Dharma.

On the contrary, if the conduct of our body and speech is unacceptable, unattractive, and coarse, not only will we not impress, we will become the object of ridicule and derision. Others will think, "So this is the way Buddhist practitioners behave," and we run the risk of tarnishing the Buddha's teachings. When we are working with others, the way we express ourselves through body and speech can have a great effect on whether things turn out well or not. Therefore, when working in groups, it is crucial that we earnestly examine our body, speech, and mind and act with great care.

The Need to Finish Work Once Begun

Whether it's major or minor, when we engage in an activity, we should reflect well on what we're doing. Without reflecting at the start, we might hastily make a lot of promises, and then when things get difficult, we might abandon this work, leaving no trace of a result, like a cloud of breath vanishing from a mirror. This is a tendency we should abandon. *The Way of a Bodhisattva* gives advice on what we should do:

> If you haven't started, that's the best.
> Once you've started, never turn back.

Measuring our energy and strength, we should examine well to see if we can accomplish a task or not. If we think it beyond us, for the time being, we should refrain from making a big commitment. In the future, when the proper time and right conditions come together, then it is all right to begin.

It is not good to start various projects, make a slew of commitments, and then be left with nothing to show for it. If there's something we think we can accomplish, we should engage in it with a totally sincere intention, attaching importance to the beginning, middle, and end. We should start out with enthusiasm and sustain our efforts through perseverance and a diligence that is joyous and delighted. In this way, we can bring a project to its conclusion.

It is said that there are three types of commitments made when engaging in any activity: one resembles an image drawn on water; another, an image furrowed in the earth; and the third, an image carved in stone. The first is unstable, the second is somewhat stable, and the third is very stable—the example we should follow. The protector Nagarjuna writes:

> Don't make a lot of promises.
> But once committed to what's difficult,
> Then like an image in stone,
> Don't change even if you have to die.

If we don't accurately gauge our ability to follow through to the end and commit prematurely to a project, we could become like the person who read Milarepa's life story and felt great renunciation. He gave up everything—his house, land, and possessions—and went into a mountain retreat to practice

Dharma. After a few years, he could not stand it and came down into town. He told the local people, "Jetsun Milarepa was so much more than a beggar, but I merely made myself impoverished." So when considering a project, we should analyze well and then make a commitment we can carry through to completion.

Fortunate ones with Dharma in their
hearts,
Plant the roots of the tree of good
intentions
In the ground of a virtuous mind
And nurture them with love and kindness.

Free of the four elements disturbed or in
decline—
The four obstacles, self-centeredness
and all the others—
The flowers and fruits of the many
qualities

Of body, speech, and mind will spread
far and wide.

In the vast space of a pure and sincere
mind
Radiates this sun of wishing to benefit
others.
The lotus flowers of the lama and
students blossom
And the bees, all limitless beings, dance.

At the request of Lama Karma Dawa from the Thrangu Dharma Center in Hong Kong, this was written at Thrangu Tashi Yangtse, set in the supreme place of Takmo Lujin (The Buddha Offering his Body to the Tigress), on the third Tibetan month at an excellent time of the waxing moon in 2011 by Khenpo Sherap Phuntsok. May virtue flourish!

About the Buddhist Flag

The cover depicts the Buddhist flag, flown throughout the world to represent Buddhism in all its forms. The flag reminds followers that there is no discrimination of race, nationality, or skin color—all beings, every single one, have buddha nature, the seed of full awakening.

The meaning of the colors has been given as follows: blue symbolizes universal compassion; yellow, the Middle Way that avoids extremes; red, the blessings that practice calls forth; white, the purity of the teachings and the liberation they bring; and orange, the wisdom of the teachings. In sum, the colors symbolize the perfection of the teachings and the great awakening to which they lead.

Michele Martin

May All Beings Be Happy